NAIRI S. GRUZENSKI

Student Quick Guide to Using The Bluebook

NAIRI S. GRUZENSKI, ESQ.

FOR LEGAL PROFESSIONALS

Student Quick Guide to Using The Bluebook

© Nairi S. Gruzenski
Porter Ranch, CA 91326
Phone 202.997.7273 • Email Nairi.Gruzenski@gmail.com

About The Author

Nairi Simonian Gruzenski is currently a practicing attorney with the U.S. Department of Homeland Security, specializing in complex litigation with the Strategic Litigation Division. Prior to joining this division, she served on DHS's Affirmative Litigation Division, and Litigation and National Security Division. While at DHS, Ms. Gruzenski was detailed as a Special Assistant United Attorney with the U.S. Attorney's Office for the Eastern District of New York, Civil Division. Ms. Gruzenski has also worked for the U.S. Department of Justice in Washington, D.C. in various roles including: from August 2005 to February 2007 as a Research Fellow for the National Institute of Corrections specifically working on writing and training of staff related to sexual misconduct in institutional settings; from February 2007 to May 2007 as a Law Clerk in the Anti-Trust Division, National Criminal Enforcement Section working on an airline price fixing conspiracy; and from May 2007 to March 2013 as a Trial Attorney with the Civil Division, Office of Immigration Litigation working on appellate immigration cases before all of the Circuit Courts of Appeal. From June 2013 to April 2014, Ms. Gruzenski was a Senior Litigation Associate at Cohen & Lord, PC in Los Angeles, California working on civil cases in California state court specifically related to real estate and construction defect. From January 2015 to October 2016, Ms. Gruzenski was an attorney with the U.S. Attorney's Office, Central District of California, Criminal Division, Major Frauds working on one of the biggest health care fraud cases. From 2022 to

2023, Ms. Gruzenski served as a Special United States Attorney for the Eastern District of New York, Civil Division. Ms. Gruzenski has been an instructor with UCLA Extension's Paralegal Training Program since April 2013 teaching mainly legal research, analysis, and writing, and has also assisted with curriculum development for those modules. Additionally, she has taught civil procedure and torts at UCLA. Ms. Gruzenski further developed an entirely new course at UCLA Extension entitled Effective Writing in Legal and Business Settings. Ms. Gruzenski has also been an instructor for Cal State LA's paralegal program where she taught legal research and writing, American legal studies, and administrative law, and helped develop curriculum. In addition to paralegal studies instruction, Ms. Gruzenski has been an adjunct professor at Glendale University College of Law where she taught appellate advocacy and moot court and taught those same courses at Loyola Law School. Further, Ms. Gruzenski served as an adjunct instructor with UCLA Law's LLM program teaching international students a course entitled Law & Communication Intensive. She earned a Bachelor of Arts cum laude from UCLA in 2002 and a Juris Doctor from the American University-Washington College of Law in 2005. Ms. Gruzenski is a member of the California and District of Columbia bars.

Table of Contents

About The Bluebook 2
Navigating The Bluebook 6
How to Cite? 12
    How to Cite to Cases 14
    How to Cite to Statutes 18
    How to Cite to Constitutions 20
    How to Cite to Legislative Material 20
    How to Cite to Administrative and Executive Materials 21
    How to Cite to Periodicals 22
    Short Form Citations 22
Introductory Signals 24
Quick Tips 27
Useful Resources 29
Student Notes 31

About The Bluebook

What should I generally know about The Bluebook?[1]

The Bluebook is the style manual that controls how American legal documents are cited in legal memoranda, briefs, pleadings, court documents, and law journals. As of the writing of this guide, The Bluebook is in the first printing of the 19th Edition.

The primary purpose of The Bluebook is to provide the proper method to cite to legal authority in order to enable the reader to locate the source material. Thus, you need to cite because you will be relying on legal authority in almost any legal document you prepare, and because you want to give your reader a quick way to locate that legal authority you are referencing.

The Bluebook is not the only legal citation manual available. In addition, there is the *ALWD Citation Manual: A Professional System of Citation*, and the *University of Chicago Manual of Legal Citation*.

---

[1] Please note that references to a textbook in this guide are to the textbook used by UCLA Extension Paralegal Students in the Legal Research and Writing Course; Deborah E. Bouchoux, Legal Research and Writing For Paralegals (9th Ed. 2020).

The state of California also has its own specific citation manual, *The California Style Manual* (often referred to as the Yellowbook), which is utilized by most California State Courts. Once you have mastered The Bluebook, all other citation manuals will be easier to use and understand.

The Bluebook remains the dominant citation authority for American Law.

Chapter 1

Layout of The Bluebook

Please note that this publication is not to be a comprehensive guide to the entire Bluebook, but a quick reference for initially learning to use The Bluebook and for the more common basic types of legal citations. Thus, this should by no means be used as a substitute for The Bluebook. You will have to crack open The Bluebook. In addition, Chapter 2 of this guide will discuss in more detail the format and organization of The Bluebook.

Let me initially mention that to begin using The Bluebook it is important to understand how it is generally organized. The format of The Bluebook is organized into specific rules and tables that each deal with certain types of legal authority. For example, if you want to know how to cite cases, there is specific rule(s) for that, and often, a table(s) with additional information regarding such things as abbreviations that should be applied. What should first be understood, however, is that The Bluebook has different sections that can help navigate The Bluebook more efficiently and quickly, and get you to the relevant specific citation information much more easily. Learning about the organization of The Bluebook will save time in locating the relevant rule(s) and/or table(s) you need to apply to a specific citation.

The Bluebook is organized into the following general sections and Chapter 2 will discuss these sections in more detail:

- **Front Inside Cover**
- **Table of Contents**
- **Blue Pages Section**

- **White Pages Section**
- **Tables**
- **Index**
- **Back Inside Cover**
- **Back Cover**

Chapter 2

Navigating The Bluebook

What is the organization of The Bluebook and how to use it?

As with any reference manual, The Bluebook will become easier to use once you know where to find the information you need for citing your legal authority properly. The Bluebook is divided into numbered rules dealing with citation of particular types of material. For example Rule 10 beginning on page 87, deals with how to cite cases.

STUDENT QUICK GUIDE TO USING THE BLUEBOOK

Do Not Be Overwhelmed By The Bluebook Format. Just Jump In and Start Using It, and It Will Begin To Get Easier.

As a quick reference, there are many free available resources, such as the ones listed at the of this guide, that you can reference if The Bluebook begins to feel overwhelming. However, this guide and any resources should not be entirely relied upon; they are helpful aids. You should always reference The Bluebook itself. Thus, you will still have to know where in The Bluebook to find the relevant rule, and begin to understand how the rules are applied. This guide will be useful for just that.

Note

If you are completely lost, the blue pages of The Bluebook is a good place to start. It is an introduction to basic legal citations and refers you to the actual rule in the white pages for more detailed explanations.

As you begin flipping through The Bluebook, you will notice that the pages have different colors, there is writing on the inside and back covers, there is an index at the very back, even the back cover has a table of sorts, there are rule numbers at the very top of each page (ex. R4), and there are tables in the back pages denoted by numbers at the very top much like the rules (ex. T10). These features are helpful in navigating The Bluebook and understanding at what type of citation rule you are looking at. In addition, you will often have to refer to multiple rules and/or tables when even determining how to cite one legal authority properly. Let us take a minute to dissect The Bluebook.

Front Inside Cover

The front inside cover is a quick reference for citations used in **law review footnotes**. Although it is unlikely you will be preparing citations for law review articles, I find the front inside cover to be helpful in quickly locating the relevant rule for commonly used citations such as cases and statutes. The front inside cover also provides some citation samples, but you want to be careful not to refer to these samples if you are citing in a memorandum or court pleading. These samples are only helpful as examples for citations used in law review footnotes.

Table of Contents

The Bluebook table of contents is like a typical TOC. However, what is particularly useful about the TOC in this instance, is that it breaks down The Bluebook by Rule and lists what each Rule discusses and the page number it begins on. Again, a good starting and reference point if you are trying to locate the particular rule for a type of citation. The TOC also carves out the blue pages section, discussed below, and again indicates what each of those sections discusses. To reiterate, if you do not know which rule you need to reference, the TOC is a good place to start.

Blue Pages Section

The blue pages section are called the blue pages because they are actually blue in color and the pages are notated by a "B" at the top, for example "B.1" The blue pages provide an introduction to basic legal citation for practitioners (those using citations in legal memoranda and court pleadings) and can give a quick overview of a rule before diving into the more detailed white pages and the rules themselves. What is nice about the blue pages is that if you need more detail regarding a particular type of legal citation it will refer you to the actual rule you need to go to in the white pages. Like the TOC, this can be a good starting off point that does not feel overwhelming and will provide concise information regarding a particular legal citation.

White Pages Section

The white pages section of The Bluebook is where the rules are located, and are designated by "R" and rule number. This is where you will find the detailed rule for a particular citation format. You will notice that in addition to the rule number at the top there will also be a brief description of what that section is about. This is helpful in determining if you are generally in the relevant rule for the citation format you are looking for. You will also notice that the rules themselves are further divided into subdivisions (i.e. R1.6). These are simply subsections that are related to the general citation format topic. For example, Rule 5 generally explains citation format for <u>quotations</u>, and Rule 5.2 discusses <u>alterations and quotations within quotations</u>.

If you started at the blue pages for easy reference, often you will be directed to the rule/white pages for a more detailed explanation of the citation format. Further, you may find that the blue pages may give the basic format, but your citation format is a little more unique or unordinary, and thus, you will need to turn to the white pages for more advanced explanations regarding the citation format.

Tables

There are several tables at the end of The Bluebook and the top of the pages are designated by a "T", specifically T1-T16. The blue pages also have tables designated as "BT." The tables typically provide information regarding abbreviations for courts or government organizations in various jurisdictions, and abbreviations for words and geographic locations. The tables you will most commonly use are listed in the chart below, with a brief explanation regarding the information contained in the particular table:

Table #	Title of Table	Description
BT1	Court Documents	Suggested abbreviations for words commonly found in the titles of court documents.
BT2	Jurisdictions-Specific Citation Rules and Style Guides	References some local court rules and a number of jurisdiction-specific manuals that provide guidance on local citation practices (these take precedence over The Bluebook).

T1	United States Jurisdictions	Abbreviations divided by federal and a of the state's jurisdictions.
T6	Case Names and Institutional Authors in Citations	Indicates how to abbreviate cases name in legal citations by abbreviating any c the words listed in Table 6.
T7	Court names	Abbreviations of court names whe cited in case citations.
T8	Explanatory Phrases	Lists the abbreviations for explanator phrases commonly used to indicate pric or subsequent history and weight c authority of judicial decisions.
T10	Geographical Terms	Abbreviations for geographical location for use in case citations among othe citations.
T11	Judges and Officials	Abbreviations of titles of judges an other officials.
T12	Months	Abbreviations for months.
T16	Subdivisions	Abbreviations for names of document subdivisions frequently used in lega citations.

Note

Remember that you made need to refer to both Rule/Rules and Table/Tables to properly complete one citation to a legal authority.

Index

The index in the back of The Bluebook is useful to locate the exact citation format you are looking for. The Bluebook index is like any other index and arranged alphabetically. The index will not provide the rule or table number, but it will direct you to the specific page where you can find the citation format for a given topic.

Back Inside Cover

The back inside cover (unlike the front inside cover) provides examples of commonly used citation forms **for practitioners** using citations in courts documents and legal memoranda. Like the front inside cover, the blue pages, and the table of contents, the back inside cover is also a nice place to start without being overwhelmed by the specificity contained in the white pages of the rules themselves. Additionally, this is a nice reference because aside from providing quick examples, the back inside cover also references the applicable rule in the white pages, as well as, the relevant blue pages associated with the citation format. Thus, the back inside cover provides comprehensive cross-references. Remember, the back inside cover is a "quick reference" for the most commonly used citations in court pleadings and memoranda, and should not be a substitute for looking up the more specific rule if the citation format you need is not referenced in those two pages.

Back Cover

The back cover of The Bluebook also provides a general, quick guide regarding the rule associated with a general citation format. Again, this, like some of the other tools of The Bluebook (back inside cover, blue pages etc.), is a helpful and simple starting point when trying to locate a citation format.

STUDENT QUICK GUIDE TO USING THE BLUEBOOK

Chapter

3

How to Cite?

T*How do I actually put together real Bluebook citations?*

he following short chart summarizes for students some of the most commonly used Bluebook rules and where to find the rule in The Bluebook. This chapter, however, will also provide more detail regarding each type of citation and provide specific examples. (Volume 2 of this guide will discuss some additional types of legal citations that are less commonly used).

TOPIC	DESCRIPTION	PAGE NOS.	RULE
Style	Typeface conventions, citation placement, signals (see chp. 4 of this guide), pinpoint citations, and other style matters.	1-9	Blue pages
Short Form Citation	Repeated citations to the same source.	13-15	B4.2; Rule 4. Also, refer to each specific type of legal authority and its specific rule.
Local Citation Rules	How to convert Bluebook examples to styles used in typical court documents.	30-51	BT2.1
Cases	Citing federal and state cases.	87-109	Rule 10
Constitutions	Citing federal and state constitutions.	110	Rule 11
Statutes	Citing federal and state statutes.	111-125	Rule 12
Legislative Materials	Citing bills, resolutions, committee hearings, reports, documents, committee prints, floor debates, and legislative history.	126-32	Rule 13
Administrative and Executive Materials	Citing materials generated from administrative agencies and other executive institutions.	133-37	Rule 14

Periodicals	Citing law reviews, newspapers, magazines and journals.	138-46	Rule 16
U.S. Tables	Official names of reporters and statutory compilations for all federal and state courts.	215-77	T.1
Abbreviations	Abbreviations for case names, court names, phrases, court documents, geographic places and regions, and periodicals.	430-74	T.6-T.16
Index	Comprehensive index to The Bluebook.	351-472	Index

Case Citations

Textbook Examples
End of Chapter 4.

How to Cite to Cases

Bluebook Rule 10 covers how cases should be cited in legal documents. Here, we will briefly cover the elements of state and federal case citations. A case citation contains the following typical elements in this order: (1) case name; (2) volume of reporter; (3) reporter abbreviation: (4) first page of case; and (5) year.

In addition, Table T.1 will be referenced quite often for citing cases as this table provides reporter names, reporter abbreviations, and citation conventions for all federal and state courts.

Due to the lag time between the Court releasing a decision and when the U.S. government publishes the case, you may have to cite to an unofficial reporter. The first option for Supreme Court cases is the *Supreme Court Reporter* ("S.Ct.") or the second option is the *United States Supreme Court Reports—Lawyer's Edition* ("L.Ed.").

Note: How To Abbreviate Case Names

Pay close attention to **Rule 10.2** regarding how to abbreviate case names in a citation. As the rule tells you, Rule 10.2.1 applies to every case name (whether in a textual sentences or in citations) and case names in citations are further abbreviated according to Rule 10.2.2. Also, pay special attention to how geographic terms and government party names are abbreviated.

- **Federal cases**:

1. U.S. Supreme Court: Official Citation

➢ When citing Supreme Court cases, you **must** cite the official reporter (*United States Reports*), unless it is not available.

➢ To cite, list the following 5 elements in order:
  o Case name (underlined or italicized) followed by a comma;
  o Volume of the United States Reports;
  o Reporter abbreviation ("U.S.");
  o First page where the case can be found in reporter; and
  o Year the case was decided (within parenthesis).

Consider the following citation example:

New York Times Co. v. Tasini, 533 U.S. 483 (2001).

2. U.S. Court of Appeals

➢ Decisions from the nation's federal courts of appeal (appellate courts) are not compiled in an official reporter. Instead, all federal courts of appeals decisions are cited in West's *Federal Reporter*.

➢ To cite, list the following 6 elements in order:
o Name of the case (underlined or italicized) followed by a comma;

STUDENT QUICK GUIDE TO USING THE BLUEBOOK

o Volume of the Federal Reporter;
o Reporter abbreviation depending on edition ("F.", "F.2d" or "F.3d.");
o First page where the case can be found in the reporter;
o The abbreviation for the circuit that issued the decision (within open parenthesis);
o Year the case was decided (within close parenthesis).

When indicating the circuit court of appeals in parenthesis, remember that they do not have subscripts and should appear like this depending on the circuit: 1st, 2d, 3d, 4th, 5th, 6th, 7th, 8th, 9th, 10th, 11th, and D.C. Cir.

Consider the following citation example:

United States v. Chen, 99 F.3d 1495 (9th Cir. 1996)

3. U.S. District Courts

➢ Decisions from the nation's district courts (trial courts) are not compiled in an official reporter. Instead, all district court decisions are cited in West Federal Supplement.

➢ To cite, list the following 6 elements in order:
o Name of the case (underlined or italicized followed by a comma;
o Volume of the Federal Supplement;
o Reporter abbreviation depending on edition ("F. Supp." or "F. Supp. 2d");
o First page where the case can be found in the reporter;
o The abbreviation for the district court that issued the decision (within open parenthesis); and
o Year the case was decided (within close parenthesis).

Spacing is important in legal citations. Notice how here there is a space between "F." and "Supp." but above there is no space between the "F." and "3d." The Bluebook examples denote where a space should be for a particular type of citation by a blue dot. Pay close attention to those dots and spacing.

Consider the following citation example:

Economou v. Little, 850 F. Supp. 849 (N.D.Cal. 1994)

Note

Where a jurisdiction's cases are published in more than one reporter, in The Bluebook the **official reporter** is always listed first and **unofficial reporters** are listed in order of citation preference.

- **State cases**:

  ➢ State cases can be cited in two ways: using a **regional reporter**, and using a **state reporter**. Most of the time, you will cite a state case using a regional reporter citation. All seven regional reporters are published by West Group (see Chp. 4, pp. 126-131 of your textbook for the regional reporter breakdown).

  1. Regional Reporter

  ➢ To cite, list the following 6 elements in order:
  o Case name (underlined or italicized) followed by a comma;
  o Volume of the regional reporter;
  o Reporter abbreviation;
  o First page where the case can be found in reporter;
  o Abbreviation for the state court where the case was decided—because otherwise you will not know what state your case was decided just by looking at the regional reporter (within parenthesis);
  o Year the case was decided (within parenthesis).

Consider the following citation example:

People v. Runge, 917 N.E.2d 940, 975-76 (Ill. 2009).

> The following pages are referred to as pinpoint citations. Typically, any given citation will include reference to the specific pages where the legal concept you are referring to can be found. See B4.1.2. If spanning more than one page use a (-) to separate page numbers. Retain the last two digits, but drop other repetitious digits. See R3.2(a).

  2. State Reporter

  ➢ If you are submitting legal documents to a state court, you may have to cite to both the regional and state reporters. These are called **parallel citations** because they refer to the same case in different reporters. Consult your state's local

rules to find out whether parallel citations are necessary.
➤ Check Table T.1 for the state's official reporter abbreviation.
➤ If parallel citations are required by local rule, cite the state reporter first and the regional reporter second.

Consider the following citation examples:

Campbell v. Gen. Motors Corp., 649 P.2d 224, 227 (Cal. 1982). (NO PARALLEL CITATIONS)

OR

Campbell v. Gen. Motors Corp., 32 Cal.3d 112, 649 P.2d 224 (1982). (PARALLEL CITATIONS)

Cal.3d-is the State (California) Reporter.

P.2d-is the Regional (Pacific) Reporter.

Note

The Bluebook lists a regional reporter as each state's official reporter.

Statute Citations

How to Cite to Statutes

Textbook Examples
End of Chapter 3.

Statutes, both state and federal, are published in books called codes. A code is systematic compilation of laws that the legislature has passed. Codes are typically categorized by title number (as in the case of the U.S. code) or subject matter (as in the case of the California Code). Bluebook Rule 12 covers how statutes should be cited in legal documents.

One of the keys to citing statutes properly is to know that you must refer to Table T.1 for the proper legal citation abbreviations for both state and federal statutes.

Note

Like case law, statutes are also published in official and unofficial publications/codes. You want to make sure to always cite to the official code first. Again, Table T.1 lists both, listing the official code first and unofficial codes are listed after in order of citation preference. (You would only cite to the unofficial code if the official code has not yet published the law.)

- Federal Statutes:

All federal statute citations should cite to the official federal code compilation, the *United States Code*. The *United States Code* is divided into 51 titles, and each title number corresponds to a specific subject area.

> To cite, list the following 4 elements in order:
>   o The title number (refer to p. 74 Figure 3-3 in your textbook for a list of titles);
>   o The code's abbreviation (typically U.S.C.);
>   o The section number of the statute (with the section symbol §); and
>   o They year of the code volume in parenthesis (*not* the year the statute was enacted).

Consider the following citation example:

8 U.S.C. § 1252 (2006)

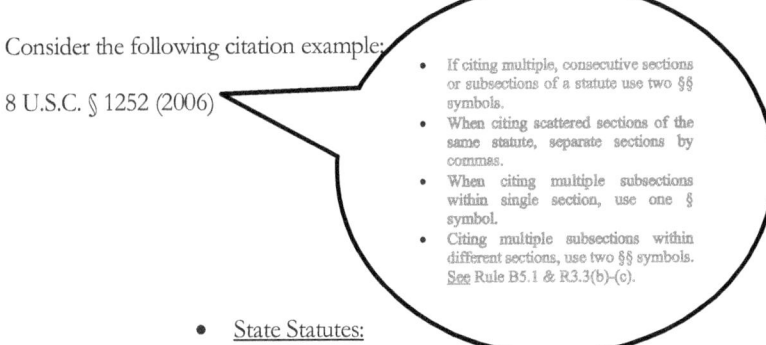

- If citing multiple, consecutive sections or subsections of a statute use two §§ symbols.
- When citing scattered sections of the same statute, separate sections by commas.
- When citing multiple subsections within single section, use one § symbol.
- Citing multiple subsections within different sections, use two §§ symbols. See Rule B5.1 & R3.3(b)-(c).

- State Statutes:

To cite to a state statute, begin by referring to Table T.1 for the particular state's statutory compilation. Each state is slightly different and may or may not have all of the following elements.

> To cite, list the following 6 elements in order:
>   o The state abbreviation;
>   o Title subject's abbreviation;
>   o The code's abbreviation;
>   o The section number of the statute (with the section symbol §); and
>   o Publisher (in open parenthesis; and
>   o The year of the code volume (*not* the year the statute was enacted) in closed parenthesis.

Consider the following California Code citation example:

Cal. Civ. Proc. Code § 581c (West 2011).

Constitution Citations

How to Cite to Constitutions

Bluebook Rule 11 deals with how to properly cite to both the federal and state constitutions. The United States Constitution should be abbreviated "U.S." and "Const." and table T.10 provides abbreviations for states when citing to state constitutions. To abbreviate the subdivisions (ie. Articles or amendments) of the constitution refer to table T.16.

Textbook Examples
Chapter 8, p. 313

- United States Constitution Example:

  ➢ U.S. Const. art. III, § 2.

- United States Constitution Example (Amendment):

  ➢ U.S. Const. amend. XX, § 4.

- State Constitution Example:

  ➢ Mass. Const. pt. 1, art. XII.

Note

The only short citation that can be used with constitutions is id.

Legislative Material Citations

How to Cite to Legislative Material

Textbook Examples
Chapter 10, p. 427

Rule 13 and Rule B5.1.6 of The Bluebook govern citation formats for Legislative Material. Legislative Material is any material put out by the legislative branch of the U.S. or a state, ie. congress. This includes all material produced prior to the bill becoming a law (statute), and produced in effort to turn a bill into a law. For example, bills, resolutions, committee hearings, reports, and congressional debates.

➢ To cite, list the following 5 elements (but not necessarily in order):
  o The title of the material;

STUDENT QUICK GUIDE TO USING THE BLUEBOOK

- o The abbreviated name of the legislative body;
- o The number assigned to the material;
- o The number of the Congress and/or legislative session; and
- o The year of publication.

Note

Abbreviations for commonly used words in legislative materials are listed in table T.9. However, if your citation occurs in text, then abbreviations are not used. For example, a senate bill would be referred to as "Senate Bill 220."

The short citation for legislative materials omits information about number of congress and date. Thus, the following short citation for the citation example to the right would be, H.R. 1731.

Consider the following federal bill citation example:

National Cybersecurity Protection Advancement Act of 2015, H.R. 1731, 114th Cong. (1st Sess. 2015).

Consider the following state bill citation example:

Immigration, S.J.R. 2, 2015-16 Sess. (CA 2015)

Administrative and Executive Materials Citations

How to Cite to Administrative and Executive Materials

Textbook Examples
Chapter 10, p. 427

Rule 14 and B5.1.4 (see also B5.1.5) of The Bluebook explain how to cite Administrative and Executive Materials. You will also need to become familiar with table T1.2. Administrative and Executive Materials are any materials put out by the executive branch of the federal or state government, or administrative decisions. This includes executive orders, Federal regulations, regulations by a specific government agency, administrative decisions, and revenue rulings. Although the rule does not give specific examples or rules for state materials, it does indicate that state materials should be cited by analogy to the federal examples given in the rule. Here are some examples of the more commonly used citations.

Consider the following federal regulation (*Code of Federal Regulations*) citation example:

8 C.F.R. § 236.16

Consider the following administrative decision (Board of Immigration Appeal) citation example:

Matter of Rotimi, 24 I&N Dec. 567, 577 (BIA 2008)

Consider the following executive order citation example:

Exec. Order No. 12,065, s 1-301(b), (c), 3 C.F.R. 190, 193 (1979

Periodical Citations

Textbook Examples
Chapter 6;
Chapter 8, pp. 349-350.

How to Cite to Periodicals

Rule 16 and B9 in The Bluebook describe how periodicals are cited. These rules include the format for citing to law review articles. Periodicals also include journals, magazine and newspaper articles, and newsletters. You will also need to refer to Tables T.10 and T.13 for abbreviations.

➢ To cite, list the following 5 elements (order may differ slightly depending on type of periodical):
- o The full name(s) of the author(s);
- o The title of the article (underlined);
- o The abbreviated name of the publication;
- o A pincite (to reiterate, a specific page number(s) and
- o The date of publication.

Consider the following law review article citation example:

Daphna Renan, Pooling Powers, 115 Columbia L. Rev. 211 (201

Consider the following newspaper article citation example:

Charles Lane, Law Curbing U.S.-Funded Attorneys is Rejected, Was Post, Mar. 1, 2001, at A4.

Short Form Citations

A short form citation may be used if you are citing the case again after you have cited it previously and used a long (complete) form citation. Rule B4.2 (blue pages) and Rule 4 cover short form citations.

Id. can be used in court documents and legal memoranda as a short form citation only when citing the immediately preceding authority; *but only when the authority contains one authority.* **See** Rule 4.1

➢ To cite the short form for a case (Rule 10.9), list the following 4 elements in order:

- o The short form name of the case;
- o The volume of the reporter;
- o The abbreviated name of the reporter; and

o The exact page where the information, legal concept, or quote is located, preceded by the word "at."

Consider the following short form federal case citation example:

United States v. Morales, 655 F.3d 608, 630 (7th Cir. 2011). (LONG FORM)

Versus

Morales, 655 F.3d at 630. (SHORT FORM)

➤ To cite the short form of a federal statute (Rule 12.10), list the following 2 elements in order:
        o Section symbol; and
        o Section number
        Or
        o The entire statute citation minus the year in parenthesis.

Consider the following citation example:

8 U.S.C. § 1252 (2006). (LONG FORM)

Versus

8 U.S.C. § 1252 OR § 1252. (SHORT FORM)

Note

Do not use "at" before a section symbol. i.e. Id. § 1252. See Rule 3.3.

➤ To cite the short form of a state statute (Rule 12.10), list the following 3 elements in order:
        o Named code;
        o Section symbol; and
        o Section number

Consider the following California Code citation example:

Cal. Civ. Proc. Code § 581c (West 2011). (LONG FORM)

Versus

Civ. Proc. Code § 581c. (SHORT FORM)

Chapter 4

Introductory Signals

How do I signify when I am not directly quoting or paraphrasing from a legal authority?

A signal sends a message to a reader about the relationship between a legal proposition, sentence or analysis and the source of legal authority cited in relation to that proposition. Aside from learning to master citations themselves, mastering the use of signals is also important in being able to cite to authorities effectively.

In non-academic legal documents (ie. memoranda and court documents), citation can be inserted into the text in one of two ways: (1) as a stand-alone citation sentence; or (2) as a citation clause.

1. **Citation sentence** (like any other sentence) begins with a capital letter and ends with a period. This type of citation comes at the end of the actual text/sentence.

    Ex. "The fact that a person is a lawyer does not make all communications with that person privileged." United States v. Martin, 278 F.3d 988, 999 (9th Cir. 2002).

2. **Citation clauses** (inserted within sentences) are set off from the text by commas and immediately follow the proposition to which they are referring.

    Ex. The Ninth Circuit upheld a district court's conduct of an in camera review of grand jury materials to determine whether the crime-fraud exception applied, In re Grand Jury Proceedings, 86

F.2d 539 (9th Cir. 1989), without disclosing those materials to the target of the grand jury investigation.

Here are a few examples of signals and how they are used with a citation.

No Signal

Use a citation after your sentence/text without a signal when:

Refer to Rules B2, B3 in the bluepages, and R1.2 in the whitepages for more information on how to use these and other signals.

- The legal authority directly states (even if it is not a quotation) the proposition.

- The sentence you are citing to is a direct quotation.

- The authority is referred to in the preceding text.

Ex. The court recognized that communications between jurors during trial "are not literally included in the prohibition of Rule 606(b) against testimony by a juror as to a statement during the course of the jury's deliberations." United States v. Kimberlin, 805 F.2d 210, 243-44 (7th Cir. 1986).

See

Use the see signal when introducing an authority that **clearly supports**, but does not directly state the proposition.

Ex. Aside from local rules, Courts have also utilized the ABA Model Rules to find that an attorney may have engaged in misconduct by initiating post-verdict contact with a juror. See Adams v. Ford Motor Co., 653 F.3d 299, 306-08 (3d Cir. 2011).

E.g.,

Use the e.g. signal when introducing an authority that is one of **multiple** authorities or jurisdictions **directly stating** the same proposition.

Ex. Other circuits have held that, while a court may inquire about premature deliberations in some circumstances, jurors may not testify about any effect the premature deliberations had on their verdict. E.g., United States v. Richards, 241 F.3d 335, 343–44 (3rd Cir. 2001) (noting that although the district court could have inquired about premature deliberations during trial, a post-verdict inquiry would violate the Rule because it would necessarily delve into the effect of premature deliberations on the verdict); United States v. Morales, 655 F.3d 608, 631 (7th Cir.2011) ("Any inquiry as to bias arising from the alleged premature deliberations would run afoul of the Rule's clear proscription....").

Introductory signals can be combined i.e. See e.g., to introduce an authority that is one of multiple authorities or jurisdictions clearly supporting the same proposition, but not directly stating.

But see

Use the but see signal when cited authority clearly supports proposition **contrary** to the main proposition. This signal essentially the opposite of when to use the see signal.

Ex. Since Bolling, it has been well established that the "Court approach to Fifth Amendment equal protection has alway been precisely the same as to the equal protection under th Fourteenth Amendment." Weinberger v. Wiesenfeld, 420 U. 636, 638 n. 2 (1975). But see Hampton v. Mow Sun Wong, 426 U.S. 8 100 (1976) ("Although both [the Fifth and Fourteenth] Amendmen require the same type of [equal protection] analysis, ... the two protectior are not always coextensive.").

Note

All signals should be underlined or italicized consistent with whether you are underlining or italicizing your other legal authorities. If you have a combined signal (ie. See, e.g.,) the underline/italics is continuous up to, but not including, the second comma. Also, you might notice the different typeface conventions. For example, in the white pages many citations use SMALL CAPS. Practitioners should always use Roman Type (NOT SMALL CAPS). See Rule B1 & R2.

Chapter 5

Quick Tips

Are there any issues with citation format I should especially keep in mind?

When to underline/italicize and when not to underline/italicize can frustrate many students. The Bluebook blue pages rule 1 (B1, pp. 3-4) cover when authors should use underlining in legal documents. Follow the stylistic guidelines in the blue pages, which are intended for practitioners. Here is a cheat sheet for the most important rules:

➢ Do Underline/*italicize*
- Case names (including the "v." and procedural phrases such as "In re")
- Publication titles
- Article titles
- Legislative history titles
- Explanatory phrase that explain prior or subsequent history (such as "cert. denied")
- Cross reference (such as "Id.")
- Any of the above that are contained in a short form citation.

➢ Do **Not** Underline/*italicize*
- Statutes
- Constitutions

- Restatements
- Reporter names
- Procedural rules

Note

According to Rule B1, publication names can be underlined OR set in italics. Underlining is the more common convention.

- ✓ With that said, be consistent within a document. If you underline – always underline- --- if you italicize – always italicize. Do not switch back and forth within one document.

- ✓ Do NOT ignore abbreviations. Each student should know where to find the appropriate abbreviations for words or names that are used in legal documents, including case names (T.6), court names (T.7), geographical terms (T.10) and periodicals (T.13). All the abbreviation tables begin on p. 430 of The Bluebooks.

- ✓ Pay attention to Table T.1 as it will be used the most. This table includes the names and abbreviations for each court, case reporter, statutory compilation, session law, and administrative code for the federal courts and the courts of every state and territory within the United States.

- ✓ Never rely on the authority itself or Westlaw/Lexis online citation formats for citing to a legal authority. Always ensure that the citation is correct according to The Bluebook.

- ✓ *As the Bluebook informs us, local court rules always trump the Bluebook. So, make sure to check the Court website when you will file your document.*

Chapter 6

Useful Resources

There are various additional resources, some free, that can be helpful to turn to when learning how to properly cite to legal authority, and here are just some examples I recommend:

1. Georgetown Law Center; *Law Library Bluebook Guide* (available online).

2. Cornell University; *Introduction to Basic Legal Citation (LII 2007)*-excellent website providing information on The Bluebook and providing examples and tutorials.

3. Linda J. Barris, Understanding and Mastering The Bluebook (2007).

4. Deborah E. Bouchoux, *Legal Research & Writing for Paralegals* (9th Ed. 2020).

5. Deborah E. Bouchoux, *Cite Checker: Your Guide To Using The Bluebook* (3rd Ed. 2010).

6. Alan L. Dworsky's, *User's Guide to the Bluebook*.

7. *Westlaw*-Cite Station.

8. *LexisNexis*-Interactive Citation Workstation (ICW online tutorial).

9. Cite-Checker App: Your Guide To Using The Bluebook (Wolters Kluwer).

10. LA Law Library--offers many affordable Paralegal Classes including; legal research, substantive legal courses, and classes on Westlaw/Lexis. (www.lalawlibrary.org/index.php/paralegal).

Federal Appellate Court Abbreviations

FEDERAL APPELLATE COURT	*ABBREVIATIONS* (note: no superscripts)
FIRST CIRCUIT	1st Cir.
SECOND CIRCUIT	2d Cir.
THIRD CIRCUIT	3d Cir.
FOURTH CIRCUIT	4th Cir.
FIFTH CIRCUIT	5th Cir.
SIXTH CIRCUIT	6th Cir.
SEVENTH CIRCUIT	7th Cir.
EIGHTH CIRCUIT	8th Cir.
NINTH CIRCUIT	9th Cir.
TENTH CIRCUIT	10th Cir.
ELEVENTH CIRCUIT	11th Cir.
D.C. CIRCUIT	D.C. Cir.
FEDERAL CIRCUIT	Fed. Cir.

Federal District Court Abbreviations

Alabama:

- Northern District of Alabama (N.D. Ala.)
- Middle District of Alabama (M.D. Ala.)
- Southern District of Alabama (S.D. Ala.)

Alaska:

- District of Alaska (D. Alaska)

Arizona:

- District of Arizona (D. Ariz.)

Arkansas:

- Eastern District of Arkansas (E.D. Ark.)
- Western District of Arkansas (W.D. Ark.)

California:

- Northern District of California (N.D. Cal.)
- Eastern District of California (E.D. Cal.)
- Central District of California (C.D. Cal.)
- Southern District of California (S.D. Cal.)

Colorado:

- District of Colorado (D. Colo.)

Connecticut:

- District of Connecticut (D. Conn.)

Delaware:

- District of Delaware (D. Del.)

Florida:

- Northern District of Florida (N.D. Fla.)
- Middle District of Florida (M.D. Fla.)

- Southern District of Florida (S.D. Fla.)

Georgia:

- Northern District of Georgia (N.D. Ga.)
- Middle District of Georgia (M.D. Ga.)
- Southern District of Georgia (S.D. Ga.)

Hawaii:

- District of Hawaii (D. Haw.)

Idaho:

- District of Idaho (D. Idaho)

Illinois:

- Northern District of Illinois (N.D. Ill.)
- Central District of Illinois (C.D. Ill.)
- Southern District of Illinois (S.D. Ill.)

Indiana:

- Northern District of Indiana (N.D. Ind.)
- Southern District of Indiana (S.D. Ind.)

Iowa:

- Northern District of Iowa (N.D. Iowa)
- Southern District of Iowa (S.D. Iowa)

Kansas:

- District of Kansas (D. Kan.)

Kentucky:

- Eastern District of Kentucky (E.D. Ky.)
- Western District of Kentucky (W.D. Ky.)

Louisiana:

- Eastern District of Louisiana (E.D. La.)
- Middle District of Louisiana (M.D. La.)
- Western District of Louisiana (W.D. La.)

Maine:

- District of Maine (D. Me.)

Maryland:

- District of Maryland (D. Md.)

Massachusetts:

- District of Massachusetts (D. Mass.)

Michigan:

- Eastern District of Michigan (E.D. Mich.)
- Western District of Michigan (W.D. Mich.)

Minnesota:

- District of Minnesota (D. Minn.)

Mississippi:

- Northern District of Mississippi (N.D. Miss.)
- Southern District of Mississippi (S.D. Miss.)

Missouri:

- Eastern District of Missouri (E.D. Mo.)
- Western District of Missouri (W.D. Mo.)

Montana:

- District of Montana (D. Mont.)

Nebraska:

- District of Nebraska (D. Neb.)

Nevada:

- District of Nevada (D. Nev.)

New Hampshire:

- District of New Hampshire (D. N.H.)

New Jersey:

- District of New Jersey (D. N.J.)

New Mexico:

- District of New Mexico (D. N.M.)

New York:

- Eastern District of New York (E.D.N.Y.)
- Southern District of New York (S.D.N.Y.)
- Northern District of New York (N.D.N.Y.)
- Western District of New York (W.D.N.Y.)

North Carolina:

- Eastern District of North Carolina (E.D.N.C.)
- Middle District of North Carolina (M.D.N.C.)
- Western District of North Carolina (W.D.N.C.)

North Dakota:

- District of North Dakota (D.N.D.)

Ohio:

- Northern District of Ohio (N.D. Ohio)
- Southern District of Ohio (S.D. Ohio)

Oklahoma:

- Eastern District of Oklahoma (E.D. Okla.)
- Northern District of Oklahoma (N.D. Okla.)
- Western District of Oklahoma (W.D. Okla.)

Oregon:

- District of Oregon (D. Or.)

Pennsylvania:

- Eastern District of Pennsylvania (E.D. Pa.)
- Middle District of Pennsylvania (M.D. Pa.)
- Western District of Pennsylvania (W.D. Pa.)

Rhode Island:

- District of Rhode Island (D.R.I.)

South Carolina:

- District of South Carolina (D.S.C.)

South Dakota:

- District of South Dakota (D.S.D.)

Tennessee:

- Eastern District of Tennessee (E.D. Tenn.)
- Middle District of Tennessee (M.D. Tenn.)
- Western District of Tennessee (W.D. Tenn.)

Texas:

- Northern District of Texas (N.D. Tex.)
- Eastern District of Texas (E.D. Tex.)
- Southern District of Texas (S.D. Tex.)
- Western District of Texas (W.D. Tex.)

Utah:

- District of Utah (D. Utah)

Vermont:

- District of Vermont (D. Vt.)

Virginia:

- Eastern District of Virginia (E.D. Va.)
- Western District of Virginia (W.D. Va.)

Washington:

- Eastern District of Washington (E.D. Wash.)
- Western District of Washington (W.D. Wash.)

West Virginia:

- Northern District of West Virginia (N.D. W. Va.)
- Southern District of West Virginia (S.D. W. Va.)

Wisconsin:

- Eastern District of Wisconsin (E.D. Wis.)
- Western District of Wisconsin (W.D. Wis.)

Wyoming:

- District of Wyoming (D. Wyo.)

Student Notes

www.ingramcontent.com/pod-product-compliance
Lightning Source LLC
Chambersburg PA
CBHW050320220526
45465CB00005B/2056